A Brief
HISTORY
of Dementia's
FUTURE

A Brief

HISTORY
of Dementia's
FUTURE

*How the **RESPITE FOR ALL** Movement
Began Changing the World by Creating
Communities of Belonging in Churches
Across the Country*

MINNIE LAMBERTH

The Respite for All Foundation
MONTGOMERY, ALABAMA

For the daughters
who honored their parents
and made this movement possible.

Holey People

How many times does the Lord say go
Out of Eden, out of Egypt, out of Sodom
Leave it quickly, leave it behind
Follow the cloud that goes before you
Out of the field, where you are watching your flock
Out of Nazareth, and take your baby
When you've gotten there, go back the other way
Tent people on the move
Taking their shelter with them
Sleeping with stones for pillows
Injuring a hip with a fight in the night
When Isaac left, he dug holes for himself
Not here, not there, the people said
Pushing him to the next
I think about that
How he always stopped to dig a hole for himself
And how we live out scripture every day
As if there are holes in the plan
Where we dug in.

M.L.

CONTENTS

CHAPTER 1

Your Guide Through This Story

Please allow me to introduce myself.

My name is Minnie.

I live a small life, and I have grown to fit into it as best as I can. I like my work, and I do that from a laptop at home. I was a self-employed writer in the marketing and communications arena for twenty-plus years, generally assisting clients from my local network. Then a new phase began.

I made a connection with a nonprofit, and I am now a projects director. I came into this nonprofit work late, as a sidekick to a whirlwind personality who lives much larger than I do. We call our annual conference Whirlwind, and if you knew her, you'd assume we named it after our leader.

We are helping churches and senior organizations create their own respite ministry for individuals living with Alzheimer's disease and other cognitive issues. We show them how trained volunteers (led by a paid director) can create places of belonging for people who are experiencing isolation following a diagnosis. These friends can come to caring, joy-filled programs for a few hours of engagement and social time — and their care partners can take a break for their own appointments or errands.

There are a lot of other things that can be explained about how the movement grew and how the ministries operate, and I'll do that shortly. But the point for now is, I

1

live a small life in Montgomery, Alabama. Yet my work has enabled me to be part of a community, and that has meant a lot to me. I move around in a city where I know people and where people know me, and that is my favorite thing — making connections at restaurants, in stores, on walking trails, at church. Being part of a community has given me a way to answer the basics of who I am, why I am here, and how I can serve.

I have seen from my own experiences that it is in community where we can find healing — even when we face circumstances where there is no cure. This underlying need was the ground on which my next phase grew.

"We are going to change the world," Daphne Johnston said when I agreed to join her work with the Respite for All Foundation. The date was December 6, 2021, and I was in my sixtieth year. She and I had taken a booth at the Sushi Café on Zelda Road to discuss a proposition — which is to say, she wanted to know if I could help her with a national initiative to promote a social model of care for individuals living with dementia.

I did not have a lot of insight in this area, but I had met Daphne when I volunteered with the respite ministry she was leading at First United Methodist Church. The program operated four days a week, from 10:00 a.m. to 2:00 p.m. During that time, people living with dementia, and trained volunteers, would come together for games, art, music, exercise, shared meals, and service projects.

Daphne had launched this program in 2012, and as word spread over the next few years, she began freely sharing with people in different cities the best practices for setting up a volunteer-supported respite ministry in their own churches. Through this experience, Daphne saw how these respite ministry concepts could be easily replicable in locations across the country, and her visionary brain cells began to ignite. She was inviting me to help promote and spread this volunteer model of care, and I was interested.

During this lunch, Daphne was also solving a problem for me. I did not have a retirement plan, per se, nor did I plan to retire. However, I'd always gotten work through my personal network. That network was made up of people who were around my age, and at some point, they were probably going to retire whether I did or not. The way I figured I needed to solve that problem would be to develop a working relationship with someone fifteen years younger than I am — someone who would still be working long enough to get me into my seventies. My answer was sitting across the table from me.

I mention all of this to say, before we started changing the world, Daphne provided something that I specifically needed: steady work where I felt the contribution I was making was of lasting value and through which I earned income. Soon enough, my own sense of community grew by leaps and bounds as I committed to spending my remaining work years creating community for others living in isolation and loneliness.

Daphne not only provided an answer for some of my needs, but I also answered a couple of hers as well — chief among them, developing a structure for her exuberance and keeping a watchful eye for misspelled words and other typos. We were two, a core, but there were many more. From all our various points of entry, one after another of us would be woven together in this movement of care for our neighbors, and this is the work I am inviting you to join.

On Sundays, ministers from all over introduce the recitation of the Apostles' Creed by saying, "Where the spirit of the Lord is, there is the one true church, apostolic and universal, whose holy faith we now declare." There is one true church. However, there are any number of earthly affiliations that are part of the worldwide and eternal Body of Christ.

Because the Respite for All Foundation works with diverse faith groups and secular entities located in different parts of the country, we work with people from a lot of different backgrounds who hold a lot of different views about a lot of different things — and these views are often firm and unyielding. Yet churches with theological and cultural differences can still follow this same model and create the same ministry that offers these same tables of belonging for people from all walks of life.

This growing movement has already reached a dozen denominations, including United Methodist, Global Methodist, Episcopal, Presbyterian (USA), Southern Baptist, Disciples of Christ, Lutheran, and others, with more to come. As it has grown, our network of respite directors from different traditions has become a wonderful picture of drawing together. And it is in that spirit that this brief history of the future is aspirational.

Respite ministry is common ground — where we recognize that everyone is dealing with something, and we accept each other just as we are. In these spaces, we restore a sense of community for people who are isolated and lonely, and, in creating spaces where neighbors can sit together and enjoy fellowship with each other, we find restoration for ourselves. My hope is for a future where tables like these are set in more and more places.

Perhaps when you are reading this, the world is at peace, and everyone is getting along with each other very well. At the time that I am typing these sentences, however, that is not quite the case. There is a good bit of dissension coming from any number of directions, and I wish there were more I could do to make things better. Unfortunately, I don't have much sway in addressing the issues of the day, and perhaps you don't either.

Like most people, I wanted to make a difference in the world. Yet, as time went by, it would be clear that making a big difference would be beyond my range of influence. Instead, I could seek to make a small difference, and wouldn't that count for something too? Think of it like dropping a pebble in a pond and making a tiny ripple in the space-time continuum. Some people leave behind buildings and endowments, but who's to say small acts of significance aren't also of lasting value?

Somewhere between heaven and earth, there's a tiny spot on the map where you are standing. You may not be able to change everything around you or even anything around you. But it is in this spot — where you are called or where you are placed — that your gifts can be used to serve others.

"I alone cannot change the world," Mother Teresa once said, "but I can cast a stone across the waters to create many ripples." These are works worth doing, and furthermore, there's a high probability that you have been preparing for a while to add your own ripple of goodness where you are.

What does the future look like?

- Diagnoses of Alzheimer's disease and other cognitive issues are adding dramatically to the epidemic of loneliness in our communities. Churches can create communities of belonging that support families living with these diagnoses.

- Respite ministry provides meaningful, hands-on engagement for volunteers and becomes a magnet for the local church in how it draws members and neighbors into service with each other.

CHAPTER 2

The Past Is Prologue

One of my writing clients, an executive coach, had shared with me the theory that we have a "career DNA." In his efforts to help others find the career that was the right fit for them, he suggested that they create a career family tree. It's no coincidence that families have multiple teachers, preachers, doctors, or lawyers in their lineage. Something within us, whether through nurture or nature, tends to lead us toward certain fields, and we should be aware of this heritage as we consider our own fields.

I could see how this premise was playing out in Daphne's case. An only child, Daphne liked to say that she grew up under a conference room table. Her mother, Barbara Mobley, worked with the Auburn University Cooperative Extension Program in Anniston, Alabama, as a county agent with home economics expertise. But that simple description hardly does justice to Barbara's rock-star status in her community. Over her years in that role, Barbara became a go-to expert in her local area on almost any home-related topic imaginable — as shown in clippings from *The Anniston Star* recounting astonishing versatility in the advice she gave to her neighbors during the 1970s and 1980s.

Let's say you'd been freezing plums, blackberries, and strawberries for two years, and now that you were ready to make jelly, you were worried about the quality of the pectin. Well, Barbara Mobley was there to tell you that, yes, some of the pectin may be weakened in the freezing process but adding commercially prepared pectin would help the fruit gel properly.

If you were interested in learning to make cottage cheese, call Barbara and she would mail you a booklet entitled "Making Cottage Cheese at Home." Or if you purchased a lot of cottage cheese at a reduced price, Barbara would tell you that cottage cheese can be frozen and offer best practices for doing so. If the biscuits you were making were always too crumbly, Barbara was there to explain that you're using too much shortening and give you a biscuit recipe that could also be altered for pancakes.

If you bought a car from a friend and wanted to get rid of the smell of his cigar smoke, Barbara was the one to ask how to do that. If you wanted to know how to upholster furniture, contact Barbara because she had some literature to help you with your project. Or if you, as a young married couple, were getting deep into debt, you could call Barbara, and she'd help you set up a budget.

Barbara conducted workshops on food preservation and omelet making along with seminars on arthritis and diabetes. She held demonstrations on testing pressure cookers, making pickled corn relish, and learning to can at home. Her typical audience reflected Daphne's future focus. "In her job she worked with senior adults all the time," Daphne recalled. "I was always with seniors."

Even more significantly, sometime around the year Daphne was born, Barbara Mobley began organizing Elder Camp for seniors in her area. Held in October at a nearby church facility, attendees loaded buses for a three-day event featuring classes on such topics as holiday treats, fraud prevention, home weatherization, first aid, beauty tips, microwave cookery, and exercise.

Daphne joined Barbara at these camps for the first eighteen years of her life — even missing three days of school because Barbara thought it was important for Daphne to be there. "Her teachers loved having her go because she would come back and tell everyone what we'd done," Barbara remembered.

"I was taking suitcases off the buses, I was in the classes, I was serving food, I was passing out the worksheets," Daphne recalled. "It is one of my fondest memories."

Through her presence at Elder Camp, Daphne became infused with the concepts of seeking purpose, staying active, maintaining health, and learning new things at any age. "This was my first experience seeing that people didn't want empty activities," she said.

Barbara was brilliant. She was named valedictorian of her small-town high school in Mississippi, where she graduated at age sixteen, and she was widely respected by the bigger names in her field. One time Daphne asked, "Momma, why didn't you get your Ph.D.?"

"You are my Ph.D.," Barbara answered. Indeed, she was. Barbara poured into Daphne the value of lifelong learning, an understanding of group activities, the instinct to encourage, the importance of community, and an orientation toward purpose.

Yet there was also another side to Daphne's career DNA. Her father, David Mobley, was a high school coach and teacher. During her student days at Donoho High School in Anniston, Daphne became a star volleyball and basketball player before continuing those sports at LaGrange College in Georgia. Her coach and mentor, Karen Hester, called Daphne a "coach on the floor" because she was always a leader for her teams.

If you could travel back in time, you would see a picture of that emerging leader the summer after her first-grade year when Daphne and her dad were walking to a nearby community center to play tennis. "There were little girls and boys everywhere," David recalled, "and they were saying 'Hey, Daphne. Hey, Daphne.' I said, 'Looks like you know a lot of people here.' And Daphne said, 'I got my reputation.'"

Surprised (and possibly concerned), her dad asked, "You got your ... what kind of reputation? How did you get it?" Daphne proudly explained that one kid in her first-grade class was picking on all the girls. But as she told her dad, "We got him to come around the corner during PE, where the teacher couldn't see him, and I got him down on the ground and sat on his chest and told him to leave the little girls alone or I was going to get him. And he did. I got my reputation."

Daphne's instinct for advocacy and protecting the vulnerable came early, and it never abated.

Many expected her to continue in her dad's footsteps as a teacher and coach. This unmistakable influence is present in how she tapped into the competitive drive and coaching instinct needed for building a national initiative. These are key traits. Otherwise, she became more closely aligned with her mother's career, especially Elder Camp where she had seen first-hand how special it was for seniors to have meaningful experiences learning in community.

"From a small child, I knew that this was what I was meant to be," Daphne said. "This is what I wanted to do with my life. I was going to be in senior care. I just didn't realize that it was going to be a ministry."

What does the future look like?

- God sets the lonely in families, Psalms 68 says. Often these families show us how we want to operate in the world (or how we don't want to operate). One way to honor this aspect of creation is to create a new sense of family for our isolated neighbors.

- Congregations have members with untapped skillsets who can be drawn into service if shown the vision. All of us want to live and serve with purpose, no matter our age, and our service to others can be transformative for our own lives.

CHAPTER 3

Church Solutions for Community Issues

Daphne earned a bachelor's degree in sociology and a master's in gerontology before beginning a fifteen-year career in the private sector as an administrator in long-term care facilities, including memory care units. "When I got married and had my family, I just couldn't keep up the 24/7 of an administrator," she recalled. "That's when my senior pastor approached me about starting a dementia ministry in our church."

Daphne was a member of First United Methodist Church (FUMC) in Montgomery, where Lawson Bryan served as senior minister from 2007 until 2016 when he was elected as a Bishop in the United Methodist Church. Early in Lawson's tenure at FUMC, the church conducted a community survey as part of its preparation for a new long-range plan. That survey was the impetus behind the launch of the dementia ministry.

"We started asking the question, 'What needs to happen in this community that will not happen unless the church does it?'" Lawson explained. "If you ask that of any community, you'll get a long list of answers. 'We're concerned about crime, concerned about education.' But this focus arose because somebody in the community in a number of different locations kept mentioning dementia."

Addressing this need made sense for a church that had earlier established what grew to be the largest counseling center in the tri-county area and had also begun a program for children with cognitive and developmental challenges. "There was a motivational match with health and healing that resonated with this church," Lawson said. It also resonated with Lawson on a personal level. "My mother-in-law lived with dementia. I knew it was a need. I didn't know what the answer could be, and so we prayed about it, not in a perfunctory way, but saying, 'Lord, what do we do with this?'"

In the meantime, Daphne was learning about other respite ministries in the Southeast — visiting locations in Lawrenceville and Columbus, Georgia, as well as in Fairhope, Alabama. One day she called Lawson to say, "I see the vision." Given her background in gerontology and senior living administration, Lawson recalled, "She was uniquely equipped to see this vision."

Before the planning of a new respite ministry was complete, the church turned again to the community for input. In August 2011, FUMC held a community forum to gauge the community's response to a proposed dementia ministry. Organizers had anticipated that a crowd of maybe seventy-five would show up for an event on a Wednesday evening. Yet more than 400 were in attendance — confirming the interest. This forum, Lawson recalled, "allowed us to say to the church, we really do need to move ahead here. The community has a need and is ready."

One of the featured speakers from that night was Dr. David Geldmacher, a professor of neurology and head of a memory care department at the UAB School of Medicine in Birmingham. "I recall the community forum in Montgomery as if it were yesterday," Dr. Geldmacher said thirteen years later. "The audience was very engaged, very positively disposed toward the message. But at the end of it, a woman approached me and practically grabbed me by the lapels and said, 'I need to tell you something we want to do here, and I want your input.' That's part of how my contributions to respite began. And that person, of course, was Daphne Johnston."

The church hired Daphne away from her senior living administration role a short time later, and she became the developer and director of the respite ministry that opened in March 2012. She started with two participants in a program led with the help of fourteen volunteers that she had trained to fill the day with joy and engagement.

"Congregational respite has been around for decades. That was not my original idea," Daphne explained. But during the year when she researched existing ministries, she mapped out the best practices of what she'd seen. "I pulled what I thought would be useful for our program in Montgomery, and that's how we built our local ministry here."

Of course, Daphne also drew on those early special memories from Elder Camp where she'd seen "that people really wanted purpose, and they wanted community, and they wanted to be together, and they wanted to grow together."

For his part, Dr. Geldmacher continued to stay aware of the benefits of respite ministry as the movement grew. "When someone walks in to see a respite program, they might see a lot of joyful, positive activities but not understand the actual value to the neuroscience in that," he observed. "We know that when people move more, that they stay healthier, that mobility is a critical aspect of well-being in people with neurologic disease."

Active games may appear fun, he noted, but they also have value in other ways. "Social engagement, being with people and positively engaged with other people provides great value for mood and mental energy for people with dementia and older adults as a whole," Dr. Geldmacher said. "When we see the volunteers participating, they are getting benefit as well from their positive interactions with each other and with the participants in the respite program."

What does the future look like?

- Respite ministry is an opportunity for a church to step in and become part of a solution to a growing need within a community — namely, support needed for individuals living with dementia-related issues.

- The planning stage for a new respite ministry is an opportunity to invite other community partners to join your congregation in this service to neighbors.

CHAPTER 4

The Secret Sauce of Volunteer Power

Have there ever been moments when you felt a prodding, a nudge, or a stirring of your heart that caused a shift of some kind — or led you to take an action? Sometimes I've been excited about a nudge of this type and felt a certainty that I was about to begin the one thing I was supposed to do with my life. The shift, change, or dream I pursued ultimately might not be as far-reaching as I envisioned, but what I would find instead is that I entered a new season of ordinary life that yielded a deeper mystery as its treasure. I was meant to do something, and I could sense it, but that something was still yet ahead.

Theologian and author Frederick Buechner famously wrote, "Listen to your life. All moments are key moments." His premise was that God speaks to us through our lives and that, if we open our eyes, we can see the "fathomless mystery" in our ordinary days. In this way, we are connected to eternity, and this notion can be of comfort — that one day we will be able to see all the moments more clearly.

Yet we are also connected to today, and it is this day that is available to us to participate in the good works being done in this world. It is in this day that we can plant a seed, water a garden, serve a neighbor, or love one another.

So it goes that the simple things you do day in, day out, are part of an eternal mystery. These simple things add up, especially when other people like you also do simple things.

And many of these simple things that you and others do become the foundation of church life in our communities.

Churches are basically the largest volunteer operations in existence. They could hardly be open for business each Sunday without dozens of individuals stepping in to provide the programming and fulfill the operational duties. Furthermore, while on one hand these volunteers are working for free, considering that they are also contributing financially to their churches as they do, they actually pay for the privilege of working for free.

This embedded system of mission-driven volunteerism is one of the reasons a church is a logical environment to launch a weekday respite ministry. They are able to enlist a slew of volunteers who have a personal desire to serve their neighbors and make a difference in their neighborhoods. People who are eager to act as the hands and feet of Christ are motivated by a vision of what is possible.

Volunteer-run respite ministries typically have one paid staff member, but the rest of the room is filled with trained volunteers who provide the fun and laughter that is medicine for the hearts of their isolated friends. Sometimes these volunteers knew a loved one who lived with dementia, and they see this as a tangible way to support others who are experiencing the same sorrows and challenges. Or they may know a friend with a new diagnosis, and they come together with this friend to spend time in a group setting. Often volunteers sign up to serve because they're responding to their own need for purpose.

The training that occurs is essentially teaching volunteers how to be a friend to someone living with dementia. The instructions are not medical but are more akin to being respectful and preserving autonomy. For starters, prospective volunteers are told not to talk down to someone but to use adult language. Don't take over an activity but prompt or guide friends as they work on an art or service project. Don't come up behind people but greet them from the front. Use language that gives purpose, such as asking questions like: "Will you sit next to Mary? She's anxious today and needs a friend." Or "Will you help me hand out the cards for our next game?"

In her training, Daphne taught volunteers how to use games and activities to connect with individuals living with dementia. For example, she conducted a group whiteboard activity where she would put a theme on a large board — something along the lines of "Celebrating the Fourth of July" — and say, "Tell me some things you think of about when you're celebrating the Fourth of July." People in the room yell out responses such as "going to the beach" or "eating hot dogs." As she explained to volunteers, don't be the first to answer but give our friends a chance to answer. Or help prompt an answer from a friend — perhaps saying, "I like to sit under something to stay out of the sun. Do you like to sit under anything to stay out of the sun?"

Volunteers also learn that respite ministry is a "no label" environment. Everyone wears the same type of name tag, and there is no distinction between volunteers and participants. "We're all dealing with something," Daphne has often said. "Why single out someone for a dementia illness?"

Doing good work like this always seems like a great idea in the abstract — someone should do that, we tell ourselves — but how do churches encourage people to make what could seem like a large commitment? Built into the principles of the Respite for All model are ways to address the hesitations people have about signing up to volunteer.

Volunteers don't have to commit for long periods of time. That is, they don't have to say, "I'll come each Tuesday for forty-eight weeks." Instead, they say, "I'll come next Tuesday." The week prior, Daphne's ministry sent out an email for the next week to ask who is coming and what day they will serve. The volunteer simply committed one week out. As Daphne often said, "There is no guilt. I do not want you running from me in the grocery store."

Just as importantly, volunteers don't have to get their own substitutes when they can't attend. Asking someone to do something that you're not going to do yourself can be uncomfortable. This is more like group volunteerism. The responsibility does not fall on one person but is spread out among many. With the number of volunteers in the pool receiving the respite ministry sign-up request, enough will usually step up to fill the slots — or else the director will know which day she has to send a second request for more people to attend.

Churches are also a logical environment because they can repurpose a fellowship hall or empty classroom to provide rent-free space to operate during the week. This is key to the respite ministry's financial sustainability. Ministries typically charge a modest tuition to cover the director's salary and food costs, but even this is less than someone would pay for a sitter for the same amount of time. Also, generous donations from the community enable churches to offset tuition for those who cannot afford to pay.

Another key factor — tuition includes a shared, hot meal where people gather with their friends around a table and enjoy nourishment together. Lunch areas are filled with plated meals, and volunteers sit at the tables to carry the conversations and to serve as mirrors to prompt their friends to eat. "A shared, hot meal is a luxury for someone living with dementia," Daphne tells her teams, and this luxury is part of the healing of these programs.

Early in Daphne's respite ministry days, she recognized that the food costs were the largest expense. Yet this expense was lessened when one of her volunteers suggested that they pay for their own meals. "I can't ask volunteers to pay for their meal," Daphne said at first. But her volunteer explained, "Daphne, we would pay for the privilege of serving here."

She began accepting volunteer contributions for their meals, but on an honor system. "I'm not chasing you down for twenty dollars, and I'm not keeping up with who pays," she explained. "There's an envelope at the check-in station where you can contribute five dollars for your meals." And that too became woven into respite ministry culture.

What does the future look like?

- Respite ministries often start with a part-time director who is included in the church staff. Directors serve as a coach for the volunteer team — building people up, finding hidden talents, demonstrating ways to improve, and addressing any issues one-on-one when needed.

- Respite ministry is a social model of care. Because no medicines are administered during the day, no medical training is needed. Instead, volunteers are caring people who can be taught techniques for engaging with individuals living with dementia.

CHAPTER 5

Expanding an Ecumenical Concept

Participants, volunteers, and support for the growing respite ministry at FUMC often came from other congregations and faith groups in Montgomery. For example, an Episcopalian congregation, Church of the Ascension, began to hold an annual fundraiser each summer, Lobsterfest, through which proceeds from the sales of lobsters were split between the respite ministry and Ascension's own ministries. Ascension also sent volunteers, as did congregations from other churches and denominations.

One of the earliest respite ministry participants was Jeanette, a member of a nearby Jewish congregation, Temple Beth Or. As Daphne recalled, one day Jeanette's daughter, Alison, was in town and came to visit the respite program where Jeanette was spending her day. Overcome by what she saw, Alison asked, "Why can't we have this in Birmingham?"

"You can! You can have it," Daphne responded quickly. She went to her office to copy the paperwork and budget she was using and handed them over. Daphne later drove to Birmingham to meet with a team from a Jewish community center that opened the first replication of the model in January 2015.

The second replication came the following January, when First United Methodist Church in Dothan, Alabama, drew on the model to open its respite ministry. At the time

Katie Holland was serving as director of a ministry for older adults at the church. She was also living with the same issues that other care partners were experiencing. "My dad had Alzheimer's," Katie explained, and as she searched for a way to support families in southeast Alabama affected by the disease, she was directed to the ministry in Montgomery.

"I went to visit, and I could not believe what I saw when I got there," Katie said. The activities — from group games and art projects to balloon volleyball — were engaging, the room was upbeat and active, and there was a lot of laughter. "I left crying. I couldn't believe how much joy was in the room."

It took about six months for Dothan's respite ministry to get off the ground, and after the program launched in January 2016, Katie recognized that the engagement of volunteers met another need. The church already offered events for fellowship for senior adults, she said, "but we didn't have a great hands-on ministry. This was something that is active and meaningful for the volunteers. They love it."

Canterbury United Methodist Church in Birmingham had also gotten word about the ministry in Montgomery and came for a visit. When Valerie Boyd joined Canterbury's staff as the director of senior adult ministries, one of the first things she did was start a support group for care partners who were caring for loved ones living with Alzheimer's or dementia. "My grandmother had Alzheimer's, and my mom cared for her for thirteen years. I saw the effects that it had on my mom and on our family," Valerie explained, noting, "This is why I do what I do."

In an earlier role at a retirement community, Valerie had started a support group and did so again in her church role. "I probably started with maybe five or six people, and after a couple of months, they kept saying, 'We need a break.

We are so exhausted. We need somewhere where our loved ones can go,'" she said. Valerie knew that the church wasn't equipped to establish an adult day care or anything along the lines of a medical model, but she soon found a better alternative in respite ministry. She got a call from a church member who told her about a program in Montgomery that was a social model program for people living with early to moderate-stage dementia. "I thought, yeah, let's go check that out."

Valerie assembled a group, and they headed south on I-65. "When I walked in respite in Montgomery, and I saw Daphne, and I saw and felt the joy and the passion and the laughter, I felt everything literally viscerally. I knew that this is what I wanted to do. I wanted this ministry to come to Canterbury, but I had no idea how I was going to do this. I felt like there's no way. I'm not smart enough. I can't do this. There's so much involved. And Daphne was the great encourager and said, 'Don't worry, I will help you every step of the way. You've got to do this. We need more of these programs. We can't just be the only one. We need this in every church. Let's do it.'" Canterbury opened its respite ministry, called Encore, in June 2016.

The snowball had begun. That same month, Auburn United Methodist Church opened a community respite program also modeled after the one in Montgomery. Daphne, it seems, was developing a reputation and in 2017 was recognized with an award given by her United Methodist Church conference which honored the contributions of women in ministry. A member of a church in Demopolis, Alabama, attended that conference session, saw the respite ministry in action, heard Daphne's story, and began the process that established the same ministry in her city in March 2018.

The quick explanation of what people experience when they visit is group energy. You might expect a dementia ministry to be sad and quiet. Yet by filling the room with friendly, enthusiastic volunteers — often at a 2:1 volunteer-participant ratio — these weekday gatherings address the isolation experienced by individuals living with dementia by providing engaging, enriching activities in a fun environment. Again, rather than a healing that is medical, the healing instead comes from being in community with others — and this healing is shared by participants, care partners, and the volunteers themselves.

What does the future look like?

- As Ecclesiastes says, there's nothing new under the sun. We can discover solutions that are already creating new life and adapt them for our own communities. Churches don't have to reinvent the wheel.

- People might expect a dementia ministry to be a room filled with sadness. Yet visiting a respite ministry in action is the best way to experience the life-giving, engaging community taking place.

CHAPTER 6

New Birth in a Funeral Home Parking Lot

In 2007, Warren Barrow was serving as an executive vice president for Caddell Construction, an international general contractor located in Montgomery, with responsibilities for managing construction projects in such locations as Sierra Leone, Mali, and Guinea. He had traveled from the camp his company had built in Freetown, Sierra Leone, to meet his wife Dolores for a vacation in Paris. That vacation, however, was not to be.

Dolores had flown from Montgomery to the airport in Atlanta, but once there, she became confused. She was able to reach Warren on the phone, and as they talked, she told him that she could not figure out how to board the flight to Paris. Thankfully, airline personnel stayed with her and helped her board a flight back to Montgomery, where her son picked her up at the airport. Warren flew home from Paris on the next available flight.

This and other symptoms that Dolores was experiencing eventually led to a diagnosis at age forty-eight of frontotemporal lobe dementia — a rare form of early onset dementia that typically strikes people ages forty-five to sixty-five. Warren and Dolores dealt with this illness on their own for several years until a visit to Dr. Geldmacher's office at UAB in 2012, where Warren learned about the respite ministry in Montgomery. "I didn't call for three months," he remembered. But when he did, he said, "It changed my life. It changed Dolores's life."

One of the practices of introducing new participants to respite ministry is to welcome them as volunteers. When Daphne met Dolores, she said, "I told her I was going to put her to work. She had been a volunteer at a hospital and was comfortable meeting people, even though she had lost her language skills."

Warren was nervous about leaving his wife with volunteers and stayed at the church with Dolores for their first few visits. But as he began to feel comfortable that she was safe and thriving, he was able to step away and get respite for himself. He also joined the care partner support group that Daphne had begun.

In December 2017, Dolores died at age fifty-eight — a sad loss of a beautiful soul. Yet in this loss a great movement began. As Daphne recalled, Warren hugged her in the funeral home parking lot and said, "I'm going to give you a significant gift because I want to see this program go all over the country."

That gift came from the sale of a beloved antique car. During her illness, Dolores' favorite pastime had been taking long rides with Warren in his 1955 Chevy — a cherry-red hot rod. Within a few months, Warren would sell that car to turn it into a financial gift to pursue this national initiative.

Warren well remembers when he and Daphne gathered in his living room with a small group of volunteers to brainstorm how they would start a foundation, what they would call it, and what their mission and goals would be. "We had paper taped all over the walls and wrote every thought we had," Warren reminisced. "The name Respite for All was born that night." This was a name that signified all three groups that were creating and benefiting from this sense of community — participants, care partners, and volunteers. Also, looking back, you can see that this small gathering of five was ecumenical from the beginning, as it included members of Methodist, Baptist, Episcopal, and Anglican congregations. These plans became official as they sought designation from the IRS, which was effective as of January 2019, when the organization was established as a 501(c)3 nonprofit.

That same year, Daphne helped launch two additional respite ministries in Birmingham, Alabama, and another in Eufaula, Alabama. In a true coast-to-coast picture of where this was headed, she also helped launch new respite ministries in Sequim, Washington, and in Sun City Center, Florida.

Rhonda Heyn, who established the respite ministry in the state of Washington, recalled, "I ran across Montgomery's respite ministry website and called Daphne and asked if I could pick her brain about how to successfully launch a ministry. She was very excited to share what she knew, so I asked if I could visit to see it in action." Eventually Rhonda was part of Daphne's first organized training for new programs. "I went down in February 2019 with a volunteer to the first director training and was able to use all of Daphne's advice to make our ministry a success," Rhonda said.

Caty Richardson, a mother with three young children who was a practicing attorney in Eufaula, Alabama, was also there that day. Her family had begun a difficult journey after her mother was diagnosed with Alzheimer's disease in 2016. The connection that led her to the training came during a visit with her parents to UAB where a nurse practitioner, Jo Ann Hackett, told her, "I want you to go back to Eufaula and your church, and I want you to start a respite care program, and I'm going to give you the name of the person who can help you do that. It will make all the difference in the world to your mom and all the people in Eufaula." As Caty recalled, "That was the first appointment that I left feeling hopeful … where I left feeling like there may be something I can actually do to help my mom live better."

Daphne's name was, of course, the name Caty had been given, and during their first phone call, Daphne told her to identify a director for the program. When Caty was unable to find someone to direct or start a respite ministry, however, she stepped up and did it herself. She set a date in summer 2019 for Daphne to come to Eufaula to train her local volunteer team and hoped, as Daphne had told her, to get forty people there. When the day came around, Caty recalled, "Sixty-five people from nine different churches walked into our fellowship hall." A few weeks later, on the first day they met as a respite ministry, six families brought their loved ones.

The Respite for All structure would continue to be fortified over the next few years, but the mission was clear from the beginning: coaching churches and organizations in best practices for launching and operating a respite ministry. "I have had many mentors and many people that helped guide me, and that's what I want to do with the Respite for All Foundation," Daphne explained. "I want to share all the knowledge we have so people don't have to reinvent the wheel. I want them to have everything at their fingertips … we want to take communities and show them how one or two churches or organizations can host this kind of ministry or this kind of program, and then we want to give them the tools to build it, and we want to show them how they can be sustainable, how it is super easy to do."

Importantly, she emphasized, "This is a social model of care. This is not medical. This is four hours. We created the 10:00 a.m. to 2:00 p.m. time slot because it was a good space for a care partner to be able to make a doctor's appointment on a Thursday when they knew their loved one was with us. They could go without someone in tow. They could go to the grocery store. They could go run errands."

Daphne continued to direct the local ministry full-time for several years while running the national initiative on the side. In the meantime, as all this expansion was taking place, I was in another part of Montgomery wondering what my next volunteer activity should be.

What does the future look like?

- Respite ministry is a replicable, sustainable social model of care that operates with one paid director and is supported by volunteer power, a modest tuition, and, frequently, community donations.

- In his poem "Manifesto: The Mad Farmer Liberation Front," Wendell Berry offers a beautiful idea when he says, "Be joyful though you have considered all the facts." And his concluding thought is simply this: "Practice resurrection." Respite ministry achieves both aims.

CHAPTER 7

Chance Encounters Open Doors

The first two years that I was self-employed, I rented an office from a friend who had set up a marketing firm in a downtown location. As his business grew and he made plans to relocate, I opted to move my work back home. This made sense to me because during those first two years, I'd only had two visitors — for an average of one every twelve months. Even then, my work was mostly done by email or phone, or I went to the client's location for whatever in-person communication was needed.

As I switched to a work-from-home arrangement, I added one thing in my business plan that I thought was needed: eat lunch out every day. With the savings on rent, gas, and clothing, I was basically reallocating funds to networking in my community. This would not only reduce isolation but would also give me a chance to be in locations where I could see people I knew at various lunch spots. My friend Jan was the one I ate with most often, and one of those lunch times with her was how I connected with the respite ministry at FUMC.

Backing up a bit, I had over the years sought volunteer opportunities to give myself a break from the tedium of work. I had discussed this idea with my former college roommate and long-time friend Lisa, a staff minister at her church, and she advised me that when I volunteer, I should do something outside my skillsets. This was a good tip. I didn't want to volunteer to write someone's newsletter, for example, because doing work for free is not a way to break the tedium of work nor would it help with the ongoing challenges of being self-employed. But I did want to have different experiences where I could learn new things, gain new insights, and develop new relationships.

During one season, I delivered cookies to homebound church members on their birthdays. During another season, I volunteered in a church kitchen serving fellowship supper on Wednesday nights. Another experience involved working in a church preschool on Sunday mornings. When I was ready for something different, I began to consider the respite ministry that I had heard about in a roundabout way.

In 2015, I was interviewing someone I knew for an article, and she told me about her husband's experience with the respite ministry that Daphne was running at FUMC. "You should go visit," Mary Ann said. "You should talk to the people there. You should see what's going on. It's a wonderful program."

It's been my experience that people often have ideas about what other people should do, but I did not see or understand how visiting this respite ministry was something that I would do. First, it wasn't my church at the time. I didn't have any contacts in the program. Furthermore, I didn't know anything about working with people living with dementia — and, accordingly, I didn't see it as a volunteer activity that would be right for me. As far as I knew, there was no door that would naturally open for me to learn more, nor would I be any good at this work if it did. But Mary Ann was insistent that I should visit, and I stored that idea for a later time.

In 2019, respite ministry had come back to mind, and I started talking about it with my friends who were members of FUMC and wondering if this was an opportunity I could pursue. The FUMC program had grown to where an assistant director, Laura Selby, led the ministry on Tuesdays and Thursdays while Daphne led the ministry on Mondays and Wednesdays. As it happens, Jan and I were eating lunch at Chicken Salad Chick, where we'd been talking about the program, when Laura stopped in to pick up a to-go lunch. As Jan saw her walk by, she said, "There's Laura now. I'll introduce you."

That's how I made my initial contact with the local ministry. I went to observe and participate on the Laura-led Thursdays. Daphne wasn't around on these days, and I did not meet her personally for several weeks.

Instead, I met people like Buddy — he no longer talked, but he still lit up the room with his presence. I found out that he'd been a theater teacher at high schools in town and an adjunct instructor at local universities. I also met Allen, a participant who'd earned his doctorate after serving in Vietnam and spent his time studying lizards, squirrels, and woodpeckers throughout his schooling and afterward. He taught biology in high schools as well as in colleges and universities.

I met a participant named Bettye, who over the course of her career had been a teacher and/or librarian at a number of schools in the area. Notably, she had been selected by the Montgomery Board of Education as one of two African-American teachers to integrate the faculty at Lee High School in 1967-68. She later worked with the Montgomery County Board of Education where, among her accomplishments, she helped introduce computer technology into school library media centers.

I saw Doris Jean again. She and I had for a short time been part of the same Montgomery Press and Authors Club that was so old Zelda Fitzgerald had once been a member. Although she was now living with a cognitive illness, she was still as friendly and cheery as ever.

Among the volunteers, I saw men who were friends of my first boss, the head of an advertising agency who hired me to become a copywriter shortly after my college graduation. This was a lifetime ago, but I had that job for five years at the start of my adulthood, and it meant the world to me. It was so nice to see these gentlemen again.

There were many others — people beloved by their families, who'd made real contributions in their careers, in their communities, and in their churches. Respite ministry was giving them an opportunity to return to community engagement, to be part of social events, to be with friends again, and to have purpose. I could see, as others had seen, that a lot of goodness was happening in the room. Furthermore, this new circle that I was in seemed to be a full circle to which I was returning. I hoped — but wasn't sure — that this circle would be open to me.

Daphne, of course, had gotten her reputation. I had heard about her and how she was the life force behind this ministry, but I didn't even know what she looked like. Then one day a woman swirled into the room like a whirlwind, and everyone was speaking to her. "Hey, Daphne, Hey, Daphne." We were introduced, and that was the full extent of that initial experience. Later, she found out about my skillsets and asked me to look over a journal article she was writing. After that, she asked me to take a look at an annual report she was preparing for the nonprofit she had established. Basically, she had a sense of how to tap into other people's strengths, and she kept turning to me for ways I could be of help.

I volunteered on Thursdays for about nine months, until the respite ministry took a break in 2020 during the

COVID pandemic. Even then, Daphne kept reaching out. Sometimes she just wanted to discuss the entertainment I was streaming. We seemed to like the same shows. Other times she had a need. I stayed involved by helping with her communications, and that's what led to our conversation over lunch in 2021.

What does the future look like?

- Respite ministry is like a backdoor to the church. Because it is a ministry for the community, people will participate who might not have considered joining a Sunday school class or attending a worship service there.

- Having found a place of welcome, non-members involved in respite ministry may choose to stay, to join a Sunday school class, to attend worship services, and to participate in the local body of Christ.

CHAPTER 8

Opening Church Spaces for Reengagement

"All streams flow into the sea, yet the sea is never full. To the place the streams come from, there they return again," Ecclesiastes 1:7 (NIV) tells us.

I don't know if the ancient Greek philosopher, Heraclitus, ever read the book of Ecclesiastes, but his memorable observation seems related: "No man ever steps in the same river twice, for it's not the same river and he's not the same man." Rivers are always moving; thus they won't be the same the next time someone enters. Also, the person who enters again has changed as well during the time that has elapsed.

Similarly, I think it's true that you can never enter the same church twice. From one week to the next, there's a different combination of people within the building. Furthermore, the individuals in that building exist in the constant of change, even as they return to what seems familiar.

When I was in my early twenties, I visited the church I had attended during my childhood and was immediately transported by the familiarity of the environment. Something during those early experiences had been internalized — not a Sunday school lesson but the sense of place I felt in the hallways, the stairwells, and the rooms in the preschool areas. Even the familiarity of the tables, chairs, and flooring awakened a *sense* of memory if not a particular memory, and I missed being part of a church.

This visit came back to mind years later when I served in a preschool Sunday school class. It seemed to me that, besides the story time and lessons, children were gaining familiarity and comfort within the church building. The essence of the buildings — carpet, tile, wood, or whatever — became part of their experience, and how they felt in these rooms and hallways was part of creating a sense of place that they might internalize and recall when they need it later in life.

I have to wonder what individuals living with dementia are experiencing when they return to the hallways and rooms of a church — rooms they might have been shying away from because of the changes in their cognitive processes. Does it awaken long-held muscle memory?

Optional worship services are part of respite ministry and are a welcome oasis for participants and families who aren't comfortable in a traditional service. Once a month or so, a thirty-minute time is scheduled for the end of the day when the care partner can come early to join in, or those who don't want to participate can leave early. The congregants sing a hymn, have communion, and offer prayers. As Daphne says, the hardest part is finding a minister who can shorten a sermon to eight minutes!

During one of the worship services she led, she recalled that a participant spoke up during a time of prayer. "People are always praying for me since I've had this illness," the participant said. "I want to ask for prayer for my family." He too had concerns about his loved ones that were weighing on his heart, and he brought these concerns into the worship service as a prayer request for others. While we don't have human measures for one person's presence in the body of Christ, we can trust that the church was changed by his return.

That's just one of the things taking place in the intentional programming of respite ministry. Verbal abilities are often a challenge for people living with dementia. Yet an engaging, twenty-minute activity during a respite day is golden for someone who is unable to speak. Daphne trains directors and volunteers on a slew of activities that help build these moments of connection. It's not about the quality of the activity, she says. It's about the opportunity to spend time together having fun.

These activities could include group experiences such as respite-style versions of Wheel of Fortune or Family Feud where the whole room joins in. There are team-divided physical games where participants and volunteers toss tennis balls into open umbrellas or toss bean bags into brightly colored buckets. Sometimes these activities are service projects — packing pet food for the furry friends of Meals on Wheels recipients, for example. Daphne emphasizes the importance of giving participants who have been leaders in their churches, career fields, or civic organizations a way to keep contributing to the community, and she reminds volunteers, don't treat a former CEO or a retired military officer like a child.

Art is another type of activity that circumvents the need to talk while allowing participants to create something of their own. Importantly, how someone creates art is neither right nor wrong; it's an activity that can be conducted without confined steps and is a nonverbal form of communication that is a safe place to express deep emotion. There are many studies that can tell you about all the benefits of art for mood and wellbeing, and Daphne often schedules an expert in this field to train directors during our annual conferences. She also reminds directors to be intentional about buying adult art supplies. Again, it's important not to treat participants like children, and even the type of supplies you purchase shows your respect for who they are.

Movement activities and light exercise are of high value as well, especially when music is added. And music itself creates many golden moments. Upbeat oldies are played in the room during games of balloon volleyball where participants use pool noodles to return balloons across a net, and each day ends with a music time for the group. Participants and volunteers are led through fun songs, such as "Take Me Out to the Ball Game," or patriotic songs, such as "My Country Tis of Thee," or traditional hymns, such as "Amazing Grace" and "What a Friend We Have in Jesus." That's what my friend Mary Ann highlighted when she first told me about respite ministry — that her husband Gene, a retired Baptist minister, loved to sing the old hymns. Like the experience of reentering a church, the muscle memories for music also return and even people who don't talk still love to sing.

In churches I've attended, it's been common to sing the hymn "Just as I Am," as if all people are welcome to come into a church building and enter a life of faith just as they are. But I think some of us have experienced enough of this mortal life to sense that humans don't always mean that or feel that. "Really?" we might ask. "Just as I am in these clothes? At this income level? With this personality? With these differences in opinions or points of view or life experiences?" Yet respite ministry is a place where "just as I am" is a real thing. People from any station in life can enjoy friendship and fellowship within these rooms.

So much in the life of faith is about turning — turning from your old life and turning toward your new life, for example, through salvation in Christ. But it's also about returning. Restoration. Reconciliation. As if we are looking for that place we once knew and are trying to find it again. Respite ministry can provide a means of return to the life of the church.

What does the future look like?

- The activities that fill a respite day are intentional. They're not about being the best or achieving success, but they are designed to create connection, movement, stimulation, purpose, and joy.

- People living with different types of dementia may lose their verbal abilities but can still connect with others through games, music, and art.

CHAPTER 9

Remembering in Community

Genesis tells us that God created humankind in His own image — starting with Adam and Eve but extending to the rest of us too. We're all created in the image of God, and this is something that doesn't change, even if we don't remember.

In his book *Ministry with the Forgotten*, Ken Carder writes about our identity as "image bearers" in the context of memory-related illness. In 2009, Carder's life as a Bishop in the United Methodist Church and as a professor at Duke Divinity School was disrupted when his wife Linda was diagnosed with frontotemporal dementia. He began wrestling not just with the losses and sorrow that entered their lives and the strains of being a care partner, but as a professor and researcher, he also began to view what was happening in their lives through a theological lens.

"We are more than our symptoms and capacities," he writes, as he explains that our identities are not what we're able to know and do or remember. That's a key takeaway from his book, but within these chapters, he also unearths the need for community to carry this identity.

When Carder talks about memory, for example, he clarifies that it's not a physical thing but is a combination of recalled events and interpretation. We remember things differently even if we have the same experience. He goes on to say that memory is communal. We are all shaped by the collective memories of families, cultures, nations, and neighbors. We carry the memories of people we have lost and hold on to them on their behalf. Plus, often in our conversations with each other, we try to remember something together.

Furthermore, Carder says, the admonition in scripture "to remember" is directed to the community. We remember the deliverance of Egypt from slavery in community. We partake of the bread and wine in remembrance of Christ in community. The chaos and exile experienced by people living with dementia is a picture of our own chaos and exile from which we received salvation in Christ, and a community response to these challenges provides restoration and reconciliation.

These are pictures of what happens in respite ministry each week. Respite ministry is communal in that it is a gathering of people who might otherwise be experiencing isolation. Respite ministry is a place of belonging for people experiencing exile. And respite ministry is redemptive as it brings new relationships and new community into disrupted lives. Daphne tells groups that it is very hard to make a new friend after a diagnosis, yet respite ministry is a place where new friendships are formed every day.

The term *re-member* has been used in sermons and Sunday school lessons by others, but it was new to me when I heard it recently. If you view the word *remember* as *re-member*, you will have a perfect analogy for respite ministry. Bodies have members, of course. And respite ministry helps us re-member individuals who have been separated by illness from the body of Christ. Through respite ministry, churches are re-membering individuals living with memory loss by restoring them to community.

I have felt re-membered myself. Since joining the Respite for All movement, I've been able to engage in productive, collaborative ministry. I've joined a mission that is larger than myself, and I'm able to attend daily to projects that, after I'm done, will still be moving forward into the future.

Early on, when I began volunteering in the local respite ministry, I wasn't particularly comfortable navigating the experience. But there was another volunteer, Norma, who was very nice to me. Norma would invite me to sit with her at her table. She always made a place for me.

With our name tags being first name only, I didn't know anything else about Norma until months down the road when we played a game called "chip on the table." This is a group activity where the respite director gives each person ten colored plastic chips and asks a series of questions. If you answer yes to any question, you put a chip in the middle of the table (like an ante). The theme that day was about meeting notable people, with the first question being "Have you ever met a U.S. president?" Norma picked up a chip and put it in the middle of the table. She'd met George H.W. Bush.

Meeting a president happens, I suppose, so I didn't think much about it. But then we moved on to college football, which is big in Alabama. The director asked, "Have you ever met Nick Saban?" He's quite well known for his success as a coach in this state, and Norma picked up a chip and put it in the center of the table. The next question was, "Have you ever met Pat Dye?" He was a famous coach on the other side of Alabama's instate rivalry with Auburn, and Norma picked up another chip. More football names continued as Norma put more chips on the table, and finally I turned to her as if to ask, "Who are you?" She simply shrugged and said, "My husband was a football coach. I've met all of them."

I didn't realize I'd been sitting next to someone who'd moved through life among prominent people and who'd been part of a lot of big events and introductions. But it didn't matter. Respite ministry is an opportunity for people with many different types of experiences to come together at the same table.

In this national initiative, my sense of belonging was fostered as I worked with the Respite for All team, board members, and directors from across the country to create more communities like this. During that process I entered a new church family myself. Along with purposeful work, that is what the connection to respite ministry made possible in my life, and like many great causes, it grew when someone said, "Here, you can sit by me."

What does the future look like?

- Respite ministry is a place of belonging for those in your community who are experiencing isolation and exile, and it is redemptive as it brings new relationships into disrupted lives.

- Respite for All's Bishop-in-Residence, Lawson Bryan, describes respite ministry as fertile ground for biblical, theological reflection and allows us to experience the theology of creation, the theology of redemption, and the theology of hope through this hands-on ministry.

CHAPTER 10

The Beauty of Problem Solving

There's something in this world that opposes good things. Even in a ministry that everyone agrees is needed, it is the nature of life on earth that if you pursue a goal, you will meet resistance, misunderstanding, conflict, competition, and/ or human error. Sometimes equipment malfunctions at the most inopportune time. Sometimes the tool you're using or the process you're following becomes obsolete, and you have to learn a new technology (hard to do!). Sometimes there are external events you could not predict that change your trajectory. Regardless of what is in the way, there are always problems to overcome.

In the book *Integrity: The Courage to Meet the Demands of Reality*, Henry Cloud, a Christian psychologist and author, writes about seeing a sign on the wall in a meeting room that said, "No problems, no profit." For Cloud, this sign answered a question for him about why the company he was visiting had experienced so much growth. "The ones who succeed in life are the ones who realize that life is largely about solving problems," he writes.

During our first year of working together, it became clear that Daphne and I both had entrepreneurial instincts. We were trying to build out an initiative in a scrappy style. One thing after another would get in the way, which is an inevitable aspect of the pursuit of good things. But we would press in, push forward, and deal with the issue. Apart from our personalities, we were a lot alike. Yet sometimes the minor difference of being complete opposites would get in the way, too. Her intensity and urgency could be slightly overwhelming on occasion. I happened to mention to her once, in the sweetest possible assessment, "Sometimes you trigger me." "I know," she said, "I know I do, but I try not to." And we went on from there.

When Daphne stepped down from her leadership of the local ministry at the end of 2022 to lead the Respite for All Foundation full time, we thought things would be easier. She'd have more time, right? Instead, things got more intense — because more people came into the mix as did bigger plans. There were more people for her to talk to, more people to get buy-in from. When I needed to get something in front of her, I'd have to find a time when she wasn't talking to five other people.

That is the nature of growth, and I could see how she was moving from entrepreneur to CEO almost overnight. She was managing multiple levels of relationships, starting with a very active and engaged board of directors.

Daphne was good at enlisting mentors. She knew how to persuade people to sign on to what she was trying to achieve. Rather than, say, choosing a board of directors solely for the financial gifts they might offer, she chose a board that provided wisdom, guidance, and experience. She chose individuals who engaged personally in the mission to spread the model. And she chose people who added qualities from their professional backgrounds in nonprofit leadership, business ownership, financial management, and so forth, as well as from their roles as respite volunteers and community leaders.

In Spring 2023, the board spent a morning working on the development of a strategic plan that included defining the organization's mission of inspiring, growing, and mentoring volunteer respite ministries. I was glad to have these words to filter decision-making. There is no shortage of good ideas, after all, but there will always be a limit on time, attention, funds, and staffing. Identifying the mission would help us make the hard calls necessary to produce the most effective results, and it brought to mind an influential memory from many years back.

In the early 1990s, when I was serving as a public information officer for a state government agency, I attended a conference for public relations professionals. During one of the breakout sessions, the speaker said, "I want everyone to write down the purpose of your job." So, everyone in the room started scribbling tasks — send press releases, keep media list current, write monthly newsletters, write speeches for the CEO, etc.

I can't remember all the tasks I wrote because so much has changed. In those days, I didn't even have a work email address. Most of us didn't have websites. There was no social media, and the media landscape was largely local TV, local radio stations, and local newspapers. This context illustrates the next point the speaker made when he said, "If you wrote down, 'write press releases,' you are going to lose your job. If you wrote down 'keep media list current,' you are going to lose your job." I was jolted to attention as he explained that those are tasks. Tasks can change. But if we remember the purpose of our jobs, and keep aligning our tasks to that end, our value in our workplaces will be stronger.

So, when the Respite for All board determined that our mission was to inspire, grow, and mentor volunteer-based respite ministries, we had identified a purpose through which our decisions could be made, and we could align our tasks accordingly.

The funding for our activities had come largely from private foundations and local donors, and this generosity was the outgrowth of a number of factors: Daphne's ability to build relationships, donors' connection to the mission, the track record of replication, as well as the support families received from their own experiences in the local ministry. We also began holding an annual luncheon in Montgomery to share tips on maintaining brain health. Daphne had learned from one of her national contacts that people want to hear how to prevent Alzheimer's disease, and we began hosting a fall event with a renowned keynote expert to provide this guidance and to introduce attendees to our mission.

Not surprisingly, Daphne was developing a reputation beyond the local area. One of her relationships came through a private foundation established by philanthropist Arthur N. Rupe, whose wife Dorothy had lived with Alzheimer's disease. A trust officer with the organization contacted Daphne to say, "We've been watching you, and we like what you're doing." She was invited to make a presentation to their board of directors, who gave the go-ahead to support the foundation's growth. Most importantly from my perspective, the Rupe organization told Daphne she could not do this on her own and needed help, and they provided the funds to bring me on board.

Our financial health was off to a good start, but we also needed to set goals and create a process so that we could continue to demonstrate effectiveness beyond our initial supporters.

By this point there were about thirty ministries in seven states in the Respite for All network, and each of these ministries had received Daphne's personal attention leading up to launch. The time she talked to the local teams and new directors, however, had often been when she was in the carpool line picking up her kids from school. Clearly that wouldn't be the most efficient way to pursue a national initiative. We needed a formal onboarding process, and that would come by adding a part-time resource director. June Jernigan, a retired member of the United Methodist Church clergy, joined Respite for All at the start of 2024, and she became the point of contact for local teams, guiding them through a checklist all the way to launch.

We also needed a formal mentoring process. The board set a goal of expanding our network to fifty ministries by 2026, and the most feasible way to reach that goal was for the existing thirty ministries to remain in operation. I recalled that one of my former marketing clients had put a lot of emphasis on customer retention. He promoted the premise that you can't grow your business by adding new customers unless you keep your current customers. Otherwise, you'll just be working to replace what was lost. Meaning that, if one or two or three of these ministries closed each year, we'd have to get back to thirty before we could grow to fifty. In a related point, since the sustainability of the model is so much a part of our message, it was helpful to show the number of respite ministries Daphne helped launch were still operating more than five years later.

Mentoring included an annual training conference for directors and volunteers, monthly online gatherings with directors, plus a private group where ideas could be shared on social media. Respite for All staff was also available to answer email questions or set up calls to coach local teams through specific issues or transitions.

Although there were fees for conference registration, a video training series, and in-person training, the mentoring was mostly provided for free. Daphne was big on operating with a spirit of generosity, and this approach was rewarded with a lot of donor support. We talked from time to time about creating a membership program for communities to join. However, we were still a staff of one full-time and two part-time people, and we didn't want to get ahead of what we were able to deliver. We opted instead to keep building value until we were ready for the next phase.

By June 2025, we had surpassed our goal for 2026. Our network had expanded to sixty ministries in eighteen states representing eleven denominations. And the vision of the future was in sight.

As respite ministries are launched in different parts of the country, they become examples for other nearby communities — and they become places for church leaders in those communities to come visit to see respite in action. For instance, the director of the respite ministry that launched in 2019 in the state of Washington helped facilitate the launch of three other respite ministries in her state over the next few years. In 2023, a senior service organization adapted the church model to launch a secular community in North Carolina, and that director has since welcomed visits from other churches and organizations in North Carolina and Virginia.

As local directors share respite ministry concepts with future communities, they connect them back to Respite for All so that we can help them launch and sustain their ministries. It has been exciting to see the development of a cohesive network, and I have been awed by the idea that people who hold the same job in different places around the country — some with years of experience, some just starting out — can all be a resource to each other for how to operate their respite ministries.

What does the future look like?

- The Respite for All Foundation team helps local communities work through the concepts of respite ministry, leads the local visioning team through to launch, and continues to serve as a resource for sustainability.

- The growing network of directors is helping generate more growth by sharing the concepts of respite ministry with other churches and organizations in their areas and by sharing their knowledge with new directors.

CHAPTER 11

Prompts of the Spirit

I remember some years back talking with a business coach who offered a simple prescription for success. Identify what you want, when you want it, and how you will get it. Basically, you set your goal and your timeframe, then put your action steps in slots on your calendar. Unfortunately, I got stuck on the phrase "identify what you want." I wasn't sure what I wanted, and without that clarity, the formula didn't work as well for me.

Determining what you want can be a spiritual question as well as a spiritual quest. In hindsight I think what I wanted was a sense of community. I surely dreamed of literary success on a national level. Yet I ultimately became a local writer who built a career through a network of personal contacts, and I have wondered if there was something foreordained in my approach. I stayed within borders not out of intent but based on the way I was led into and through this work. Perhaps it was that I brought the need to belong into my career, and the way I designed my work is what that looked like.

As I proceeded through life, I did not begin a family in my own house but instead was part of the extended family of nieces and nephews that came through my three siblings. Furthermore, I operated with contradictions. My exterior personality was shy and quiet. My interior personality was not. In adulthood, I moved through the world making connections, pursuing goals, and seeking community, but I was also a bit of a recluse.

Participating in a local church was a helpful antidote to my personal nature, and I do think being part of a church body is one of the best ways to organize life on earth. It gives you a way to learn teachings from Scripture and to grow as a disciple of Christ. It gives you an opportunity to join with others in service of a greater good. It gives you a place to try untested talents. It gives you a structure for your week. It also gives you a community where you can meet people you might have never known otherwise and, through that experience, develop rich and enduring relationships. Church membership gives you something to belong to.

I do want to point out, in the gentlest sort of way, when you've been in church rooms for long enough, you'll know they can sometimes be like a holiday meal with complicated family members or a workplace with a wide mix of personal qualities. In other words, with all due respect to the divine encounters available to each of us, church is actually a very human place to be.

I mentioned earlier that I volunteered in a church kitchen serving fellowship supper on Wednesday nights. This was a nice gig for a long while. I liked being a co-laborer, and I especially liked sitting at the worker table with the other volunteers where we ate our own meal together after our work was done.

But there were always issues. For example, I think it would have been universally acknowledged during that time that the head of the kitchen at the church I attended had a mercurial temperament. A force of nature in her own right, she held the job until the month before her ninetieth birthday and even then was still driving her red Mustang to church. All in all, the meals she prepared for Wednesday night supper were good, but sometimes she didn't filter her comments.

The reason I ended up there is because I had heard an announcement during a worship service that the kitchen needed workers. I liked that it was countcrintuitive since I don't cook and don't practice hospitality, and I thought, yes, I should try that. When you have an inspired moment where you think God is prompting you to go volunteer in the church kitchen, you follow through, right?

So, I talked with a staff member, my friend Patty, about volunteering for church supper. On the day I was to begin, I stopped by Patty's office, and she sent me to the kitchen to say I was there to help. But when I walked into the work area to announce my arrival, the head of the kitchen took one look at me and said, "We don't need you."

Well, that was confusing. I returned to Patty's office and told her that the head of the kitchen had said, "We don't need you." And Patty spoke words of prophecy right on the spot. "Yes, she does. She just doesn't know it. Let me go talk to her." Together we walked back to the kitchen, where Patty told me at the door "wait here" while she entered to smooth the way for my opportunity to volunteer.

When Patty came back out, she explained that the head of the kitchen had agreed "for tonight" to let me restock the forks and knives after the members came through the serving line. And that's what I did — diligently, I might add. When everything seemed to go okay during my trial, I was in for another week. Later, I moved on to handing out desserts, and over time I became what you might consider an essential worker on that small team. Like most people in the kitchen who survived the initiation period (some didn't!), I grew to love and accept our mercurial boss — and vice versa.

As I said, there were always issues. Even so, for a long while, sitting at that worker table sharing a meal with other volunteers was one of the best seats I'd ever had in a church. While at that table, I heard stories about people's lives and experiences, and that led me to write a series of articles that I shared on social media. That's how I ended up talking to Mary Ann who told me about the respite ministry at FUMC and suggested I visit. All I'm saying is, if I hadn't gotten past that initial encounter, my life would be very different today, but I don't know in what way.

The world is carried forward by regular people responding to prompts of the spirit, and there are always obstacles. But if you think you're hearing "we don't need you" or "we don't need this," consider these words of prophecy instead: Yes, they do. They just don't know it.

In the Respite for All movement, we call the person who begins the process a champion — the one who champions the cause. It doesn't just happen. It takes one person who says, "We need this." That person goes to another person or a church or an organization, and says, "We need this." Someone starts the conversation and keeps that conversation going, and we walk alongside them as they move toward launch.

One day as I was looking at our locations, I noticed a significant connection. As I pointed out earlier, someone whose mother was a participant in the respite ministry in Montgomery was the champion who led to the creation in 2015 of CJFS CARES in Birmingham, the first replication of this model. As time went on, another daughter, Katherine, was the champion who helped launch a location at her church in Tuscaloosa, Alabama — a mission she pursued after her father Glen began participating in the respite ministry in Montgomery.

I highlighted Bettye as one of the people I met during my volunteer days. When she and her daughter, Rochelle, moved to Kansas to be near family, Rochelle worked with a senior service agency to open a Respite for All location there, and that agency has since opened two other locations in that state.

I also mentioned Doris Jean. On visits to see her parents, her daughter, Jeanne, had observed how interactive and engaging the program was, noting that it provided a socialization that her father could not match at home. She soon began talking with church leaders and ministers at John Knox Presbyterian, her church in Greenville, South Carolina, about seeing a respite ministry launched there. From start to finish, the idea took about seven years to come to fruition — through presentations to church leaders to plans for a fundraising rollout to a COVID delay. She was the one, she recalled, "kind of getting the conversation going and keeping it going." And she ultimately prevailed, helping to open the first location in her state in 2024.

Four daughters whose parents were in the respite ministry in Montgomery helped start respite ministries in four other cities and two other states, and that is a beautiful testimony to the value of this model. When people decide to take these steps so that others will have what their families received, that is how a movement grows.

What does the future look like?

- The Respite for All Foundation casts the vision and shares best practices for launching and sustaining a respite ministry. But it takes a local person to begin the process by saying, "We need this." The champion starts the conversations and keeps the conversations going.

- Lawson Bryan describes respite ministry as an example of asset-based community development. "The community has a need, and when it comes to dementia, the church has what the community needs. Churches have space, and churches have caring people, and churches have a biblical theology that equips them for this ministry."

CHAPTER 12

Volunteers Grow in Discipleship

Who among us has the authority to become a minister? If you're talking about formal recognition, different denominations answer that question in different ways, with whatever caveats are deemed necessary for their circles of faith. Yet it is God who calls people to His work. God calls people to be the church where they are.

When I worked in state government all those years ago, I taped a quote from Archimedes on the computer screen in my office: "Give me a place to stand, and I will move the earth." I didn't know who Archimedes was or why he made that statement, but I liked how he spoke to my longings and my fears. Something within me said there was something I could do with my life that would be right for me. But I didn't know what or where or how. Over time, I came to realize that finding a place to stand doesn't have to be some distant goal. You can stand right where you are and start moving.

In that sense, respite ministry is a place to stand. It's a place to create movement in your community, a place to act in service to others. And a lot of people are finding unexpected rewards — regardless of how they enter.

Daphne originally launched the respite ministry at FUMC with the goal of giving care partners a break. That was the initial need around which the ministry was developed. Then, as the ministry continued, it became apparent that participants benefited from the physical, mental, and social stimulation offered in these loving, nurturing environments. Participants were able to act as volunteers themselves, to help others, to find purpose.

But other outcomes were also happening in the lives of volunteers. Dementia diseases are progressive, and there is usually a time frame for when participation has a benefit. Care partners and participants are here for a season. Yet some volunteers have chosen to stay involved for years, and they are providing the continuity and creating the community that is holding the memory of those who came before them.

One time Daphne was approached by a donor who gave her a large check. When she saw the amount, she asked, "What's this for?" The donor began her explanation with a simple phrase, "Daphne, I'm a bird watcher." She went on to say, every year she took a trip with a group of her fellow bird watchers, and usually the conversations between bird sightings were about family issues, grandchildren, whatever topics came up. But this particular year, her friends had been volunteering with respite ministry, and their conversations had changed. They were saying things like "I wonder how Bill is doing today. I wonder if he was able to come. I wonder if Jane is there. Sam looked really good last week. Did you see how Mary did such and such?" The volunteers were thinking about and talking about the friends they'd made in respite ministry, and the bird watcher took notice. Although she couldn't join her friends in volunteering, she did want to support the ministry in her own way.

In the Spring of 2024, Lawson Bryan and a retired educator, John Bell, led a group of long-time respite ministry volunteers through a six-week Bible study based on Ken Carder's book, *Ministry with the Forgotten*, and they conducted a research project about the impact volunteering in respite ministry had on their own spiritual lives. Among the takeaways, as volunteers used words like love, joy, patience, etc. to describe the gains from their experiences, Lawson and John couldn't help but recognize that these qualities are essentially the "Fruit of the Spirit" from Galatians 5. Their research showed that volunteers were transforming into disciples, and what better outcome could there be for church programming?

When I was a teenager, at my mother's suggestion, I read "The Great Stone Face" by Nathanial Hawthorne, and the short story has stuck with me ever since. An image carved in a nearby mountain is a continuing source of speculation among townsfolk who've heard a prophecy that one day their town will be visited by a man who looks like this image. Over the years, some will come through and take a shot at the claim. But not Ernest. He's the villager who's waiting. And watching. And wondering. In the meantime, he's also busy. He has tasks to do and duties to fulfill, and he gets them done — even as he waits, watches, and wonders about who that stone image represents.

Eventually Ernest grows old, and it's then that the townsfolk start to notice — he, of all people, resembles that image on the mountain. Ernest is the one who made a difference in their town all along. Ernest is dismissive of this suggestion, however, and he still waits, watches, and wonders.

The point comes to mind that Ernest became what he beheld; the person he watched for is the person he grew to be.

I also think often of a folk tale entitled "Stone Soup." This is where a hungry stranger comes to town and offers to make a big batch of soup out of a stone. It's an obvious scam, yet it's as if he becomes a Pied Piper of cupboard ingredients. As he swirls the hot water in a big pot in the center of town, villagers are intrigued and begin to add what they have from their own wares. As each person contributes carrots, potatoes, meat, or what have you, the soup truly becomes a bountiful meal that everyone shares.

There are lessons there as well — besides the one about being careful when letting strangers talk you out of your household goods. Because if you look beyond the trickery, you also get a picture of what happens in your community when each person thinks creatively about what he or she might bring to the table.

We often admire certain gifts and attributes in others but don't always realize that these are things we actually possess ourselves. The stone face in the mountain serves as a reminder that we all bear an image of Someone we want to be more like. And the stranger making soup stirs within the crowd a call to service that motivates us to bring our best to the town square. In that sense, serving in respite ministry is a place for each of us to become the church we want to see.

What does the future look like?

- By creating a space for ministry *with* instead of ministry *to* participants, respite ministry creates a community that has an enriching impact on the lives of all involved — participants, care partners, and volunteers. As others witness this impact, they take notice and are drawn in.

- Respite ministry is an opportunity for volunteers to grow in discipleship through hands-on, sacrificial service that is so meaningful it keeps them coming back for more. Caring volunteers create the community that carries the memories of their friends.

CHAPTER 13

The Spirit Still Moves Across Creation

I was born in Old Russell Hospital in Alexander City, Alabama, in 1961. Old Russell Hospital wasn't the actual name of that place, but by the time I was old enough to be aware of my surroundings, Old Russell Hospital had been torn down and replaced by New Russell Hospital on the outskirts of town. On drives through town in those early years, my mother would point out this area of significance. "Old Russell Hospital was over there. That's where you were born."

I would look quickly through the car window to see where "over there" was, but I never could figure it out. "Where?" I would ask. "Over there," she would explain again. Her pointing in a certain direction was not enough for me to find the answer I was seeking, however. This was perhaps the beginning of an awareness that there was a knowledge outside my understanding, and I could sense it, but I couldn't quite put my finger on it.

Somewhere within my heart, spirit, and memory, I was probably thinking of a moment like this as I wrote a novel and introduced the narrator looking through a car window on the way to her brother's ballgame. When a spectacular sight my alter-ego, Hannah, believes she has witnessed turns out to be less than she envisions, she has to reckon with that missing piece. "In one moment I was convinced I had seen the Second Coming; in the next, I was at the concession stand buying a hot dog, vaguely aware of the presence of knowledge and the absence of clarity," Hannah says.

That was a fictional line but a real feeling along my long journey.

The first stop in my writing career was a high school radio show, where I helped write scripts that my classmates and I recorded for a local broadcast. We'd visit a radio station during the week to prepare a program that was aired on Saturday mornings — for a small audience, no doubt. But this was the first time I was able to use puns and word play to deliver information in a public format. I liked it, and I started getting the idea that I wanted to be an advertising copywriter when I grew up. Somehow this became the name of my dream job in the future.

The second stop of my writing career was when I was an English major at Huntingdon College in Montgomery and wrote stories with puns and turns of phrases for the campus newspaper. After graduation, I pulled together my clippings from that paper, compiled them into a portfolio, and took them to interviews with local ad agencies. When I was finally hired as a copywriter, I called home to share the good news with my mother. In her excitement, she said, "Cast your bread upon the waters, and it comes back buttered."

My mother was a teacher and an intellectual. She wasn't known to say platitudes, but this was a big day for me, and the expression stuck out. I later discovered that the phrase comes from a verse in Ecclesiastes 11: "Cast your bread upon the waters, for you will find it after many days." In that verse, there is the idea to keep casting, keep trying — and there will be a good result.

During the mid-1990s, while I was figuring out the process of becoming self-employed, I was also writing the novel I mentioned, which was about a young girl growing up in a southern neighborhood. As I would explain in talks, there were two themes: one was a girl and her dog, because my narrator Hannah was very concerned about her beagle Pumpkin and keeping a watchful eye. The other was a girl and her God because she felt an early call to God's service and was wondering how to express that call. It was my character's intention, at age seven, to become a preacher when she grew up. The setting was 1972, and this would have been an unusual idea at that time, but that's what I wrote. I didn't think I had a call to ministry personally, but, again, that's what I wrote.

For years, sending out that manuscript felt like casting bread upon the waters. The route to publication was indeed a long one — a pursuit lasting nearly a decade that reached its conclusion when I won a contest for an unpublished literary novel with Christian themes. I thought I had arrived. I thought I had reached a pinnacle. But what I had reached was another stopping point on a journey where I continued to seek the place I belonged.

Maybe we are always trying to finish the work God began in us, even when we don't see things clearly here on earth. Lawson loves to quote Wendell Berry's character, Jayber Crow, where he says, "And yet for a long time, looking back, I cannot escape the feeling that I have been led — make of that what you will." I have felt the same.

Automotive icon Lee Iacocca made the observation, "I've always found that the speed of the boss is the speed of the team." Same here. I've witnessed the speed of Respite for All, beginning with a question Daphne asked me during that lunch at the Sushi Café: "Can you start today?" Working with Daphne has been like riding a fast-moving train on a railway that's still under construction.

Or, as we sometimes say, we're building the bridge as we cross it.

I have reflected on these analogies in terms of my own career DNA. In the early 1900s, one of my great-grandfathers was a contractor who built roads, bridges, and railways in the Southeast. He was part of creating a transportation infrastructure — at least the part that was land based — that moved large groups of people from one place to another, that connected them to each other. Working on the infrastructure for the Respite for All movement has given me a way to build another type of bridge to the future.

Related, I suppose, I'd heard that this particular great-grandfather "became senile" as he aged. I don't know what his diagnosis would have been (he died in 1946), but I do know this was an earlier description for Alzheimer's and dementia-related diseases.

In Daphne's case, she began a respite ministry in 2012 built largely from her mother Barbara's influence, and years down the road, Barbara was diagnosed with vascular dementia, one of the many cognitive issues that bring participants to respite ministry. She is still her same sweet, encouraging self — still a shining light for those around her — but sometimes her brain causes her confusion. We may not be able to change what is happening. But when our friends and loved ones begin questioning their own thought processes, we can create environments and fill them with people they can trust and where they can continue to serve.

I believe that the reality we see and experience is not the only one there is. There is another one where there is a God who watches to see what we will do. He was watching when a county extension agent in Anniston, Alabama, planted a seed in her daughter's heart that grew and grew and grew, and just like Barbara, we have options too. Among them, we can live in service to others. We can speak life and hope and love into difficult situations. We can use our lives to be a source of healing. And we can be trustworthy in a world where people don't know who to trust.

What does the future look like?

- Lawson Bryan often shares the Howard Thurman quote: "Don't ask what the world needs. Ask what makes you come alive and go do it because what the world needs is more people who come alive." Respite ministry helps create new life for all involved.

- With this new source of life, respite ministry creates vitality within the local church. As church members become involved in hands-on ministry, they can see for themselves the transformation taking place in people's lives, and they will often continue to invest themselves even more deeply.

CHAPTER 14

Is There a Respite Ministry in Your Future?

During our pivotal meeting, Daphne and I talked about the training conference she was planning for directors and volunteers from a network numbering just over twenty at that point. We discussed how we needed a legend — a tale of some type that signifies what this movement is. She's big on big moments, and we wondered what kind of symbolic gesture we could offer to open the conference that we could continue every year.

When I was back home, I thought of a story I'd heard about the author Robert Louis Stevenson that would be a good fit for our mission, and I wrote a piece to explain this concept. As a boy growing up in Edinburgh, Scotland, in the 1800s, Stevenson was a sickly child who spent a lot of time watching the activity on his street from the view of his bedroom window. The work of the leeries who came around each day at dusk to light the gas lamps became a fascination to him, and legend has it, one evening he said to his mother, "Look at that man punching holes in the darkness!"

This quote has been used often to describe the work of ministry, and it's an especially good fit for respite. We can't undo the losses that individuals and their loved ones experience when Alzheimer's and other dementia-related diseases darken their world. But we can punch holes in that darkness and let the light of love and friendship shine through.

These thoughts have since been woven into the lamplighter legend that we read as our annual conferences begin. A selected person lights a lantern on the stage, and we keep the lantern lit during our gathering.

We're not only shining a light in the darkness through respite communities, but in another sense, we also offer the lantern as a beacon to draw more people into this movement. Over the last several years, the conference has grown to include attendees from four states to six states to nine states to seventeen states, and we're keeping the light on for more.

Daphne came up with our original tagline — "Reclaiming Joy Together" — to emphasize that respite ministry enables us to step back from the sadness that diagnoses bring to families and enter into the shared joy of rooms filled with fun activities. Similarly, the growing network is joining this effort to reclaim joy, and the tagline has been echoed in the inspiring names being chosen for the new ministries that are launching. Anchor, Connections, Abide, Side by Side, Living Well, Living Spirit, and Joyful Place are some of the examples of how the Respite for All movement is reshaping how we talk about care for our neighbors. The point is to avoid calling a ministry anything that suggests "dementia day program" but helps give care partners and friends an opening to encourage participants to attend a fun and meaningful gathering. The community names themselves are other indicators of the light and laughter being shared.

The Montgomery respite ministry started with two participants and fourteen volunteers, then grew from two days a week to three and eventually four. And word spread. "People would come from miles around to find out how we did it," Daphne said. That was the organic growth.

Now the Respite for All Foundation's growth is intentional and continuing as we keep looking at how we can refine the methods we employ to inspire, grow, and mentor respite ministries. In that sense, the title of this book, *A Brief History of Dementia's Future*, tells you how we got here but is open to the unknowns of where we will end up. That could depend on you and others like you, and it's my hope that you will also help Daphne spread this model.

This is where I step aside and let you step in. I invite you to join us in creating places of belonging in your towns and changing the world one community at a time. The need is urgent. Can you start today?

What does the future look like?

- Respite for All is a name that speaks to respite for the care partner and respite for the person living with a cognitive disease. But it also encompasses respite for the volunteer and the transformation that comes from finding purpose and meaning in hands-on service.

- In respite ministry, you can bring your own gifts to the table. You can be the church for someone else. You can remember those who feel forgotten. You can be the solution you are looking for. And you can do so with the confidence that many others have already traveled this road.

To learn more about starting a respite ministry in your community, please visit RespiteforAll.org.

Into the Field

Into the field I went to look for God
Perhaps he had hidden himself there
As others talked of all his deeds
I trod a good distance, I did
But I could not find him in the field.

Into the river I went to look for God
Perhaps he had been swept away
In the currents of the day
But I could not last a minute
Before I sputtered back to the bank.

Up the mountain I went to look for God
Perhaps he had situated himself there
To see all that was happening
But I stumbled on the rocks
And slid back down to the parking lot.

How far could I be from the true good thing
I weighed the wonder as I settled into restless slumber
When the morning's commotion stirred my attention
Trucks revving for work, old men talking on the sidewalk
Into my neighborhood I went to look for God.

M.L.

ACKNOWLEDGMENTS

I would like to thank the members of the Respite for All board of directors, past and present, for encouraging and supporting this national movement. I would like to thank Slats Slaton for the cover design and Cindy Bryan for the editorial help on this project. And I would like to thank Daphne Johnston for changing my world by inviting me to lunch.

ABOUT THE AUTHOR

Minnie Lamberth is a graduate of Huntingdon College and is the author of *Miss Bertie Explains the Beginning of the World* and other works of fiction. She lives in Montgomery, Alabama, where she has enjoyed a long career as a writer for marketing and communications projects. Today, she devotes her time and energy to the mission of the Respite for All Foundation.

www.ingramcontent.com/pod-product-compliance
Lightning Source LLC
Chambersburg PA
CBHW062011040426
42447CB00010B/1999